# Stephen Hawking

© B. Jain Publishers (P) Ltd. All rights reserved. No part of this book may be reproduced, stored in a retrieval system or transmitted, in any form or by any means, mechanical, photocopying, recording or otherwise, without any prior written permission of the publisher.

Published by Kuldeep Jain for B. Jain Publishers (P) Ltd., D-157, Sector 63, Noida - 201307, U.P
Registered office: 1921/10, Chuna Mandi, Paharganj, New Delhi-110055

Printed in India

# Contents

- 5   Who is Stephen Hawking?
- 6   Birth of Stephen Hawking
- 8   Early Life and Background
- 10   Childhood of Young Stephen
- 15   Hawking as a Student
- 18   His Disease
- 26   Career and Marriage
- 34   Research on Black Holes
- 39   A New Companion—Speech Synthesizer
- 43   Hawking as an Author
- 50   Appearances in Mass Media
- 52   Space Travel
- 56   Timeline
- 60   Activities
- 62   Glossary

# Who is Stephen Hawking?

Stephen Hawking was a world-renowned British quantum physicist, cosmologist, author and director of research at the Centre for Theoretical Cosmology in the University of Cambridge. He is known for the remarkable contributions he had made to the fields of cosmology, general relativity and quantum gravity, especially in the context of black holes.

# Birth of Stephen Hawking

Stephen William Hawking was born on January 8, 1942. It was the 300th death anniversary of Galileo, the noted physicist. Hawking was the eldest child of Frank and Isobel Hawking's four children. He was born in Oxford, England, into a family of thinkers. His Scottish mother had earned her way into Oxford University in the 1930s. It was a time when very few women were able to go to college. His father, another Oxford graduate, was a respected medical researcher with a speciality in tropical diseases.

Stephen Hawking was born at a time when both his parents were struggling with their finances. The political scenario was also tense, as World War II was going on and England was dealing with the hazards of German bombs. In an effort to seek a safer place, Isobel returned to Oxford to have the couple's first child. The Hawkings had two other children, Mary (1943) and Philippa (1947), while their second son, Edward, was adopted in 1956.

# Early Life and Background

The Hawking family, as one close family friend described them, was an 'eccentric' lot. Many a time silence prevailed during dinner time as each of the Hawkings would immerse themselves into reading books. The family car was an old London taxi, and their home in St. Albans was a three-storey fixer-upper that never quite got fixed. The Hawkings also housed bees in the basement and produced fireworks in the greenhouse!

In 1950, Hawking's father took a job to manage the Division of Parasitology at the National Institute of Medical Research, and spent the winter months in Africa doing his research. He wanted Stephen, his eldest child, to take up medicine as a field of study. However, from an early age, Stephen showed a passion for science and the sky. This was evident to his mother. She, along with her children, often stretched out in the backyard of their home on summer evenings to stare up at the stars.

She remembered, "Stephen always had a strong sense of wonder. And I could see that the stars would draw him."

## Childhood of Young Stephen

When Stephen was just two weeks old, he escaped death when a neighbour's home was destroyed during the war by a V2 rocket, which also damaged the Hawkings' home while they were away. After the war ended, Hawking grew up in the historic and upper class areas of England. He went to private schools and then to Oxford as his parents had.

As a child, Stephen was awkward, skinny and puny. Clothes often hung from his body oddly, making him appear messy as he was very thin. He also had a slight lisp. His teachers found him to be bright but not much above the other students, while in elementary school. He lacked dexterity in his hands, but still did his three hours of homework every night.

As a young boy, Hawking loved to create games with his friends. They would gather and play the games on weekends and holidays at Hawking's home. Hawking would create many rules that were so complex that the games would take hours to finish; in fact, one turn could last an entire afternoon!

Hawking loved board games, and he along with a few close friends, created new games of their own. During his teens, Hawking, along with several friends, constructed a computer out of recycled parts for solving rudimentary mathematical equations.

Hawking, along with his sister Mary, who loved to climb, also devised different entry routes into the family home. He remained active even after he entered College at Oxford University at the age of 17. He loved to dance and also took keen interest in rowing.

# Hawking as a Student

In the year 1950, the Hawking family moved to St. Albans, Hertfordshire, where Hawking received his early education from St. Albans School. It was while studying here that he was recognized as a bright, but not an exceptional, student. During his first year at St. Albans School, he ranked third from the bottom in his class. However, Hawking focused on pursuits outside the school. By his own account, Hawking did not put much time into his studies. He would later calculate that he averaged about an hour a day focusing on school, and yet he did not really have to do any more than that.

During his schooling years, Hawking was inspired by his mathematics teacher and he decided to study the subject in the university. However, at that time Oxford did not have a mathematics teacher and hence did not offer the course. Hawking therefore applied for natural sciences and developed interest in thermodynamics, relativity, and quantum mechanics.

After completion of his B.A. degree from Oxford in 1962, Hawking joined Trinity Hall, Cambridge, where he studied theoretical astronomy and cosmology.

In 2008, Hawking indicated that he was certain of the existence of an alien life in various other parts of the universe; not only on other planets but perhaps on stars or even floating in outer space. He stated his belief that some of these species may be intelligent and thus may pose a threat to Earth. According to him, humans should try and avoid alien species rather than try to establish a contact with them.

# His Disease

When he was still in Oxford University, Hawking started developing symptoms of Amyotrophic Lateral Sclerosis (ALS)— a disease characterized by rapidly progressive weakness, muscle atrophy and respiratory difficulties. The first symptom of the condition appeared when Hawking once lost his balance and fell down a flight of stairs, hitting his head. On quite a few occasions he would trip and fall, or slur his speech.

Initially, the doctors believed that Hawking would not survive more than three years. He gradually lost the use of his arms, legs, and voice, and he continues to remain almost completely paralyzed even today. A Cambridge scientist built a speech-generating device, that enabled Hawking to write onto a computer with minor movements of his body, and later a voice synthesizer to speak what he typed.

Despite his illness and with the help of his doctor tutor Dennis William Sciama, Hawking continued with his PhD from Cambridge. His principal fields of research remained theoretical cosmology and quantum gravity.

On his part, Hawking never took serious note of his physical problem until 1963, during his first year at Cambridge. For the most part, Hawking had kept these symptoms to himself. However, his father took notice of the condition and forced Hawking to see a doctor. For the next two weeks, the 21-year-old college student made his h ome at a medical clinic, where he underwent a series of tests.

"They took a muscle sample from my arm, stuck electrodes into me, and injected some radio-opaque fluid into my spine, and watched it going up and down with X-rays, as they tilted the bed," he once said. "After all that, they didn't tell me what I had, except that it was not multiple sclerosis, and that I was an atypical case."

Eventually, doctors did inform the Hawkings about what was ailing their son. He was in the early stages of Amyotrophic Lateral Sclerosis (ALS). In simple terms, the

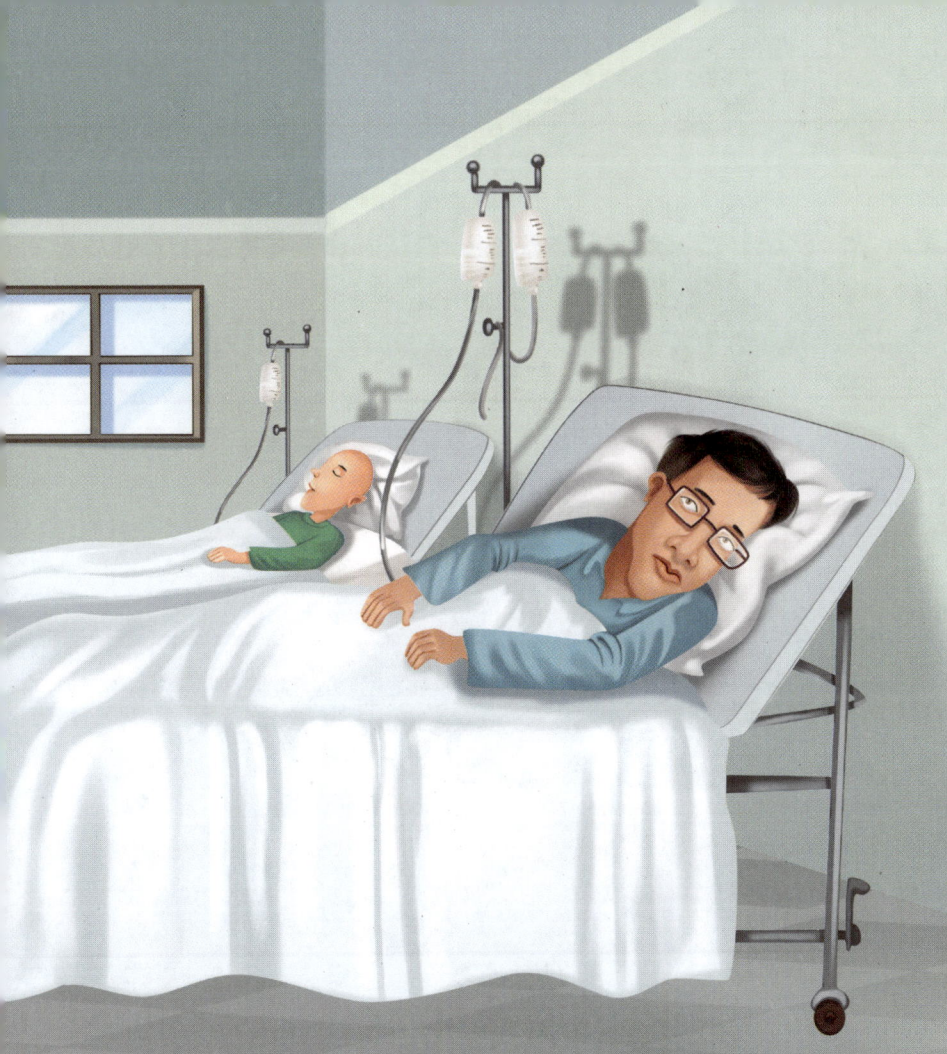

nerves that controlled his muscles were shutting down. Doctors gave him two to three years to live.

It was a shocking news for Hawking and his family. Nonetheless, a string of events helped him overcome this shock and enabled him to see some light at the end of the dark tunnel. The first of these events came while Hawking was still in the hospital. There, he shared a room with a boy suffering from leukemia. Relative to what his roommate was going through, Hawking later reflected,

his own situation seemed much more tolerable. After he was released from the hospital, one day Hawking had a dream that he was going to be executed. He said this dream made him realize that there were still many things to do and much more to achieve in life before his time ran out!

In a sense, Hawking's disease helped him become a noted scientist. Before the diagnosis of his deadly disease, Hawking had not really focused on his studies. "Before my condition was diagnosed, I had been very bored with life," he once stated. "There had not seemed to be anything worth doing."

With the sudden realization that he might not even live long enough to earn his PhD, Hawking dedicated himself wholeheartedly into his work and research.

## Career and Marriage

When Hawking attended Oxford on a scholarship, he focused on mathematics and physics as he showed a strong interest in theories. He focused on the theory of relativity of Einstein and the study of cosmology, which deals with the bending of space and space as related to time.

The year 1963 proved to be a turning point for Hawking as, on the very first day of the year, he met his future wife Jane Wilde. Soon after, he began undergoing tests, which diagnosed him with ALS. As the doctors warned that he might not live beyond two more years, Hawking was naturally depressed. However, while dating Jane and

attending his work at the college, he was able to use his mind without any signs of illness. He walked with the help of a stick and eventually had to take the help of a wheelchair. His speech was soon affected by the illness. It had become considerably slurred.

While working to receive his PhD and make a name for himself at the school, Hawking was able to handle great levels of theoretic equations in his head. At the age of 23, he received his PhD.

In 1965, Hawking decided to tie the knot with Jane. In December the same year, they travelled to Florida for a conference. As Hawking's speech was difficult to understand, a friend who had come from Texas to attend the same conference, agreed to speak for him. Robert, their first son, was born in May 1967. By 1970, Jane gave birth to their second child, Lucy.

On the career front, most of Hawking's research work on black holes was done with Roger Penrose, a mathematician who wrote the equations as Hawking communicated with them while they worked together during several years on their theory.

Hawking continued at Cambridge after his graduation, serving as a research fellow and later as a professional fellow. In 1974, he was inducted into the Royal Society, a worldwide fellowship of scientists. In 1979, he was appointed 'Lucasian Professor of Mathematics' at Cambridge, the most famous academic chair in the world (the other holder was Sir Isaac Newton, also a member of the Royal Society).

Over the course of his career, Hawking studied the basic laws governing the universe. He proposed that, since the universe boasts of a beginning (the Big Bang), it is most likely to have an ending also. Working with fellow cosmologist Penrose, he demonstrated that Albert Einstein's Theory of General Relativity suggests that space and time began at the birth of the universe and they end within black holes, which implies that Einstein's theory and quantum theory must be united.

## BIG BANG THEORY
### METRIC EXPANSION OF SPACE

The Big Bang theory is an effort to explain what happened at the very beginning of our universe. Discoveries in astronomy and physics have shown beyond a reasonable doubt that our universe did in fact have a beginning. Prior to that moment there was nothing; during and after that moment there was something: our universe. The big bang theory is an effort to explain what happened during and after that moment.

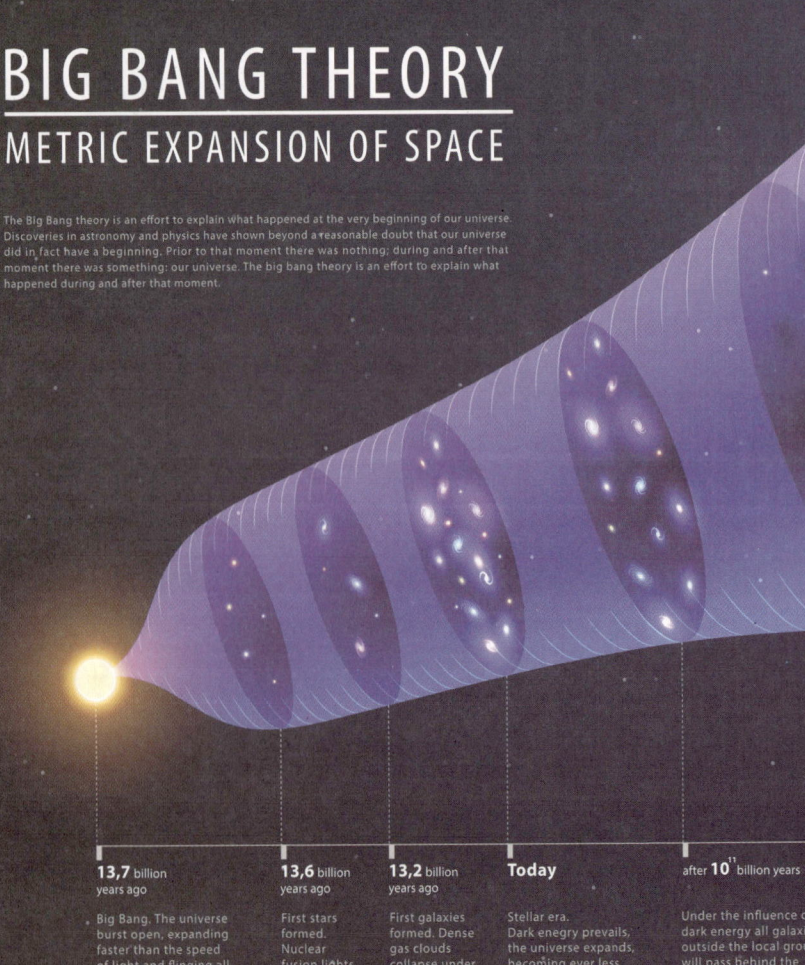

**13,7 billion years ago**
Big Bang. The universe burst open, expanding faster than the speed of light and flinging all the matter and enegry in the universe apart in all directions.

**13,6 billion years ago**
First stars formed. Nuclear fusion lights up the stars.

**13,2 billion years ago**
First galaxies formed. Dense gas clouds collapse under their own gravity to eventually form galaxies.

**Today**
Stellar era. Dark enegry prevails, the universe expands, becoming ever less dense.

**after $10^{11}$ billion years**
Under the influence of dark energy all galaxies outside the local group will pass behind the cosmological horizon.

Using the two theories together, Hawking also determined that black holes are not totally silent but instead emit radiation.

Hawking also proposed that the universe itself has no boundary, much like the Earth. Although the planet is finite, one can travel around it (and through the universe) infinitely, never encountering a wall that would be described as the 'end'.

after $10^{14}$ billion years

Star formation ends, leaving all stellar objects in the form of degenerate remnants. Black holes dominate the universe.

after $10^{40}$ billion years

The only organized units are black holes, but even black holes are unstable and evaporate into electrons and positrons.

# Research on Black Holes

Groundbreaking findings from Penrose, about the fate of stars and the creation of black holes, tapped into Hawking's own fascination with how the universe began. This set him on a career course that reshaped the way the world thought about black holes and the universe.

In 1968, a year after the birth of his son Robert, Hawking became a member of the Institute of Astronomy in Cambridge. While the physical control over his body decreased day by day and he was forced to use a wheelchair by 1969, the effects of his disease started to slow down.

The next few years were fruitful ones for Hawking. He published his book, the highly technical *The Large Scale Structure of Space-Time* in 1973 with G.F.R. Ellis. He also teamed up with Penrose to expand upon his friend's earlier work.

In 1974, Hawking's research turned him into a celebrity within the scientific world when he demonstrated that black holes are not the vacuums that scientists had thought they were. This announcement sent shock waves of excitement through the scientific world. Hawking was at once on a path that was marked by awards and distinguished titles. He was named a fellow of the 'Royal Society' at the age of 32, and later earned the prestigious 'Albert Einstein Award', among other honours.

Teaching at various prestigious colleges and universities also followed at this time. One was at Caltech in Pasadena, California, where Hawking served as visiting professor, making subsequent visits over the years. Another was at Gonville and Caius College in Cambridge.

# A New Companion— Speech Synthesizer

Hawking's ever-expanding career was accompanied, however, by his ever-worsening physical state. By the mid-1970s, the Hawking family had taken in one of Hawking's graduate students to help and manage his work. He could still feed himself and get out of bed, but virtually everything else that he did required assistance. In addition, his speech had become increasingly slurred, so that only those who

knew him well enough could understand what he was trying to say. In 1985, he lost his voice for good, following a tracheotomy—a situation that required 24-hour nursing care for the acclaimed physicist.

It also started affecting Hawking's ability to do his work. The predicament caught the attention of a California computer programmer, who had developed a speaking programme that could be directed by head or eye movement. The invention allowed Hawking to select words on a computer screen that were then passed through a speech synthesizer. At the time of its introduction, Hawking, who still had use of his fingers, selected his words with

a handheld clicker. Later, with virtually all control of his body gone, Hawking directed the programme through a cheek muscle attached to a sensor.

Through the programme, and the help of assistants, Stephen Hawking continued to write at a prolific rate. His work included numerous scientific papers and also information for the non-scientific community.

# Hawking as an Author

Hawking authored several books on the basis of his findings. His first book, *A Brief History of Time,* was first published in 1988 and it became an international bestseller. In the book, Hawking aimed at communicating questions about the birth and death of the universe to the average people. Although the book was a short one in terms of

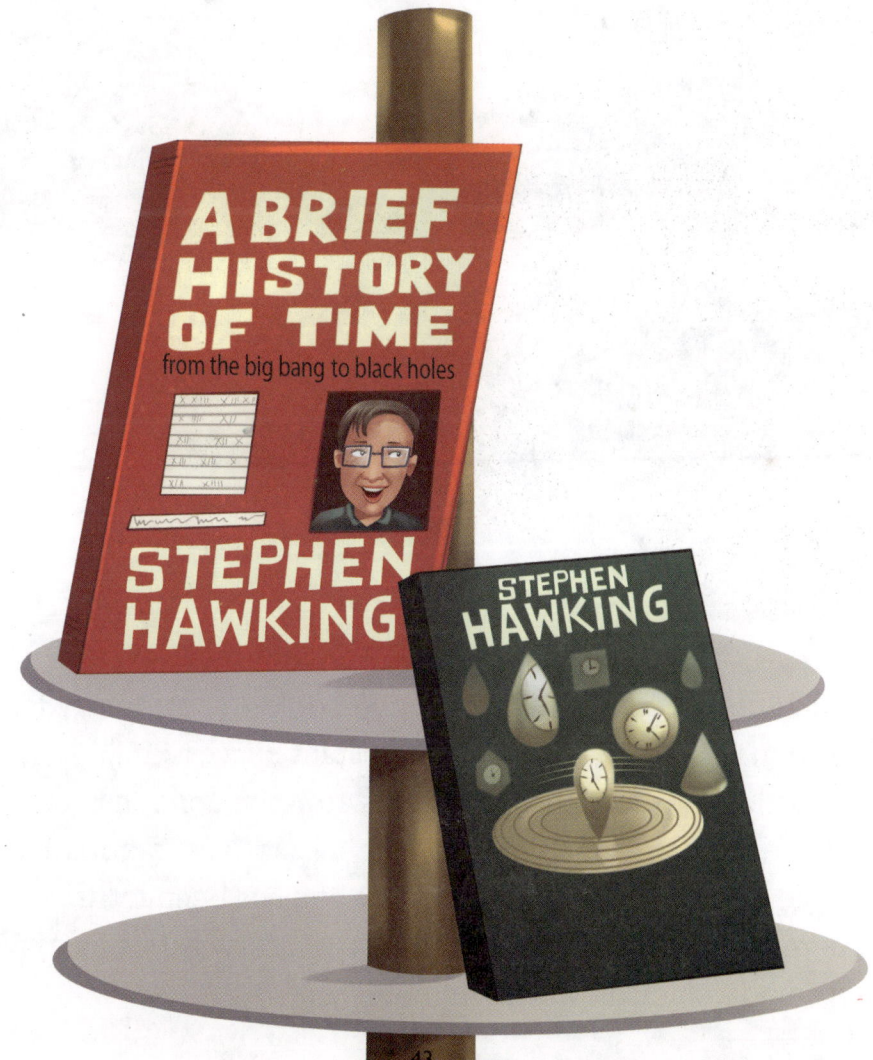

volume, it became an informative book on cosmology for the masses. The work was an instant success, enjoying a position for more than four years atop the London Sunday Times' best-seller list. Since its publication, the book has sold millions of copies worldwide and has been translated into more than 40 languages. But it also was not as easy to understand as some had hoped.

Since then, Hawking went on to write other non-fiction books like *A Briefer History of Time*, *The Universe in a Nutshell*, *The Grand Design*, and *On the Shoulders of Giants*.

He, along with his daughter, Lucy Hawking, also created a fictional series of books for middle school children on the creation of the universe, including *George and the Big Bang*.

Together the books, along with Hawking's own research and papers, expressed the physicist's personal search for science's Holy Grail—a single unifying theory that can combine cosmology (the study of the big) with quantum mechanics (the study of the small) to explain how the universe began.

It was this kind of ambitious thinking that allowed Hawking, who claimed he could think in 11 dimensions, to lay out some big possibilities for humankind. He was convinced that time travel is possible!

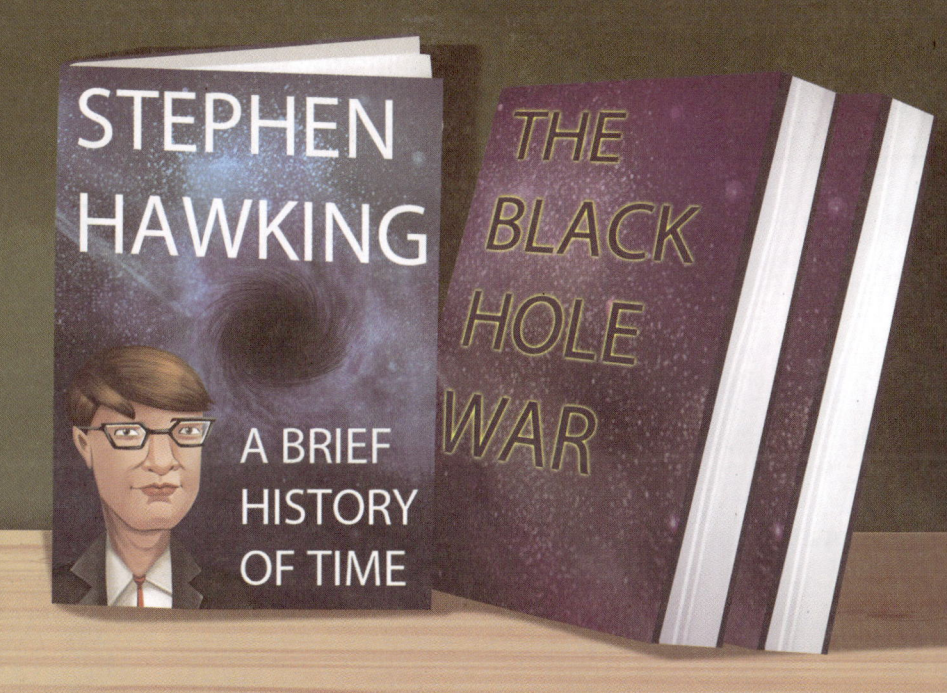

Hawking wrote books and articles, which were published on a scientific level; beyond most people's understanding level. His ALS created many difficulties, but his mind was hard at work to define how the universe was created, what all a black hole can do, and where do things go once they enter the black hole. He was also trying to define what can escape from the surface area of a black hole, that they are not truly black inside, and that black holes rotate and are also non-rotating.

Hawking redefined how we look at space, energy and the connections within many of life's ideas. He did this all within his mind and overcame not only ALS but the awkwardness of childhood and the acceptance of science in a time when society was changing drastically. He is said to have kept his humour through it all.

In September 2010, Hawking spoke against the idea that God could have created the universe, in his book *The Grand Design*. Hawking had previously argued that belief in a creator could be compatible with modern scientific theories. His new work, however, concluded that the Big Bang was the inevitable consequence of the laws of physics and nothing more. "Because there is a law such as gravity, the universe can and will create itself from nothing," Hawking said. "Spontaneous creation is the reason there is something rather than nothing, why the universe exists, why we exist," he added.

*The Grand Design* was Hawking's first major publication in almost a decade. Within the domain of his new work, Hawking set out to challenge Sir Isaac Newton's belief that the universe had to have been designed by God, simply because it could not have been born from chaos. "It is not necessary to invoke God to light the blue touch paper and set the universe going," Hawking said.

Hawking made news in 2012 for two very different projects. It was revealed that he had participated in a 2011 trial of a new headband-styled device called the iBrain. According to an article in *The New York Times*, the device was designed to 'read' the wearer's thoughts by picking up 'waves of electrical brain signals', which are then interpreted.

# Appearances in Mass Media

Hawking made several television appearances, including a playing hologram of himself on 'Star Trek: The Next Generation' and a cameo on the television show 'Big Bang Theory'.

The Big Bang Theory is a popular comedy about a group of young, geeky scientists. Playing himself, Hawking appeared in several episodes of the sitcom and delivered some delightful jibes, directed especially at the theoretical physicist Sheldon Cooper (Jim Parsons). Hawking earned kudos for this lighthearted effort.

In 2014, a movie based on Hawking's life was released. It was called *The Theory of Everything*. The film drew praise from Hawking himself, who said it made him reflect on his own life.

*The Theory of Everything* stars Eddie Redmayne as Hawking and encompasses his early life and school days, his courtship and marriage to Wilde, the progression of his crippling disease, and his scientific triumphs.

Hawking wrote on Facebook in November 2014: 'Although I'm severely disabled, I have been successful in my scientific work. I travel widely and have been to

Antarctica and Easter Island, down in a submarine and up on a zero-gravity flight. One day, I hope to go into space.'

# Space Travel

Hawking was scheduled to fly to the edge of space as one of Sir Richard Branson's pioneer space tourists. He said in a 2007 statement, 'Life on Earth is at the ever-increasing risk of being wiped out by a disaster, such as sudden global warming, nuclear war, a genetically engineered virus or other dangers. I think the human race has no future if it doesn't go into space. I therefore want to encourage public interest in space.' Hawking's quest for truth regarding

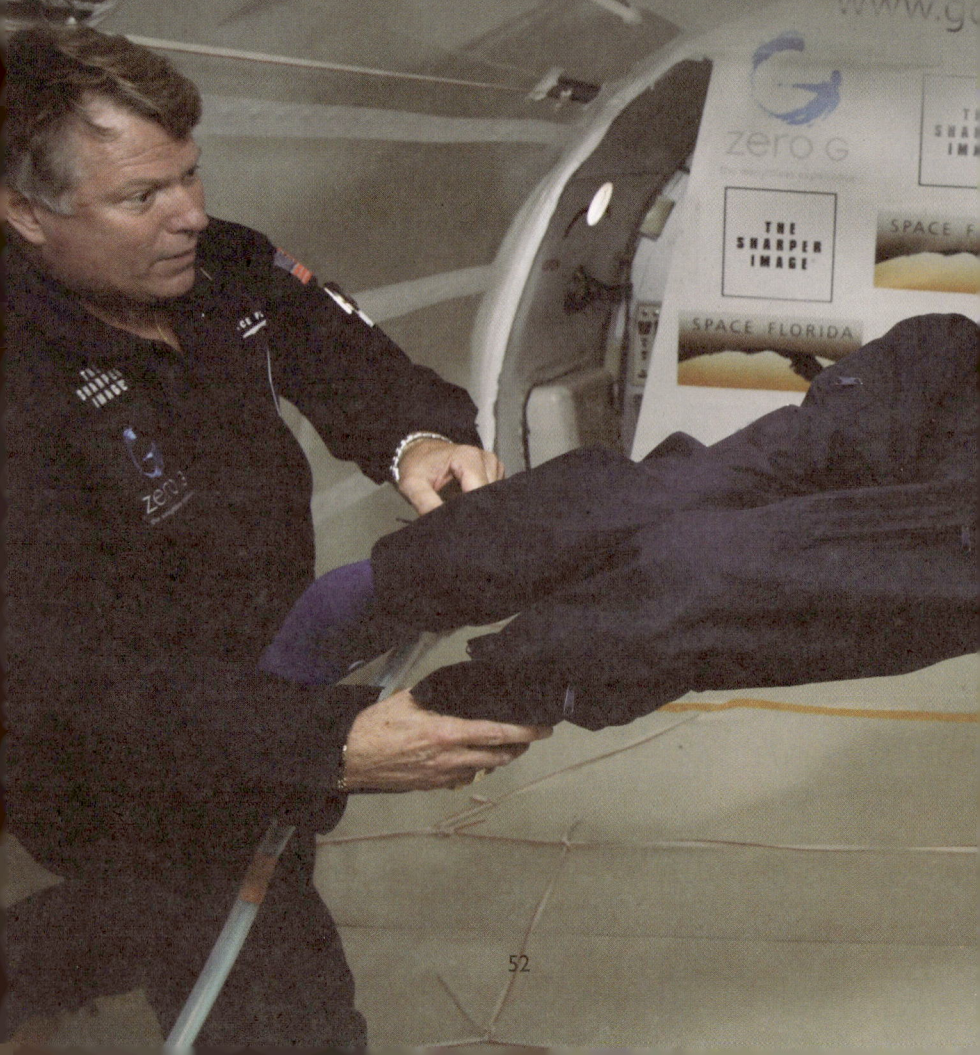

space included his own personal desire to travel into space. In 2007, at the age of 65, Hawking made an important step towards space travel. While visiting the Kennedy Space Centre in Florida, he was given the opportunity to experience an environment without gravity. In the course of two hours, over the Atlantic, Hawking, a passenger on a modified Boeing 727, was freed from his wheelchair to experience bursts of weightlessness. Pictures of the freely floating physicist splashed across newspapers around the globe.

"The zero-G part was wonderful, and the high-G part was no problem. I could have gone on and on. Space, here I come!" he said.

Hawking was a true embodiment of a rock-star scientist! He made guest appearances on *The Simpsons, Star Trek: The Next Generation,* a comedy spoof with comedian Jim Carrey on *Late Night with Conan O'Brien,* and even a recorded-voice-over on the Pink Floyd song 'Keep Talking'. In 1992, Oscar-winning filmmaker Errol Morris released a documentary based on Hawking's life, aptly titled, *A Brief History of Time.*

In spite of all these glittering events, Hawking's health remained a constant concern. In April 2009, Hawking, who had already announced he was retiring after 30 years from the post of Lucasian Professor of Mathematics at Cambridge, was rushed to the hospital for being what university officials described as 'gravely ill'. It was later announced that he was expected to make a full recovery.

Hawking lived with all physical deformities studying, researching and enlightening the scientific world. He died on March 14, 2018 at the age of 76, at his home in Cambridge.

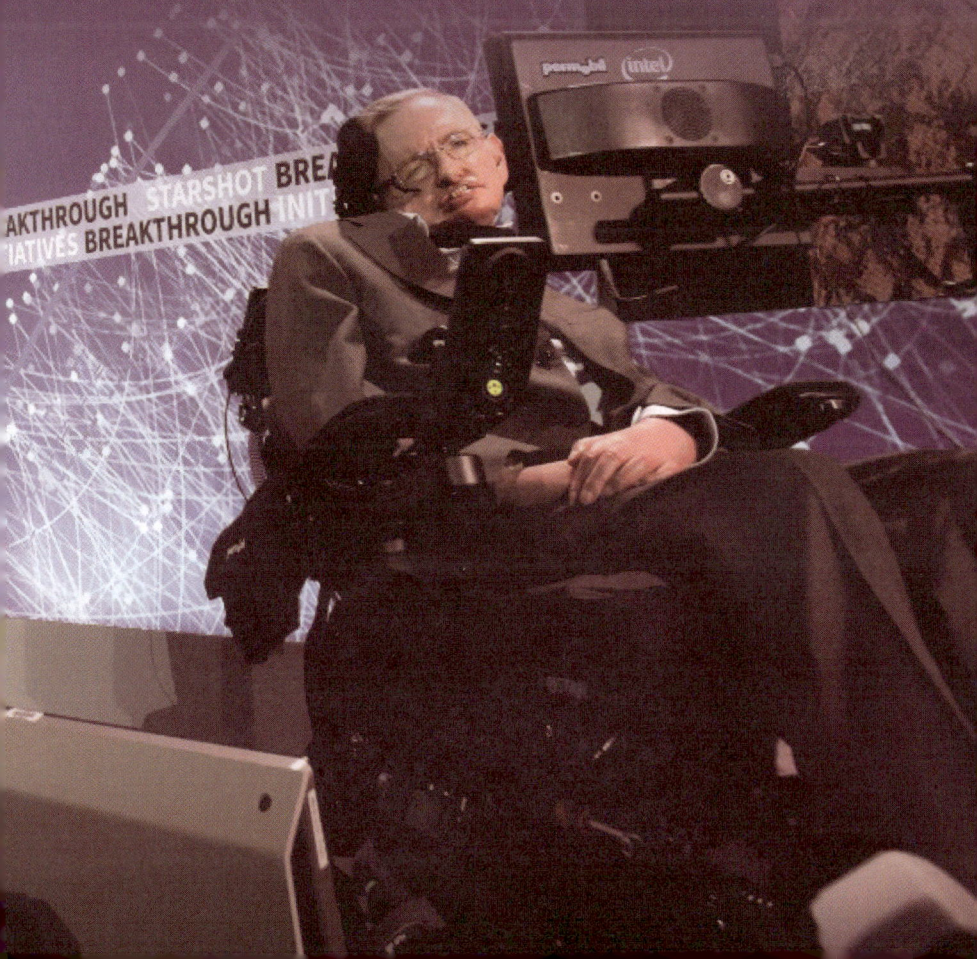

## Timeline

- **1942** Stephen is born on January 8, in Oxford, England (300 years after the death of Galileo).

- **1953 to 1958** attends St Albans school in North London, where he develops a passion for mathematics. His father wants him to study medicine.

- **1959 to 1962** specialises in Physics at University College Oxford. Graduates with a first class degree in natural sciences

- **1963** begins research in cosmology and general relativity at the University of Cambridge. He is diagnosed with an "incurable disease" at the age of 21 known as Amyotrophic Lateral Sclerosis

- **1966** completes his doctorate and is awarded a fellowship at Gonville and Caius College, Cambridge

- **1970** discovers a remarkable property: by using quantum theory and general relativity he is able to show that black holes can emit radiation

- **1973** joins the department of applied

mathematics and theoretical physics at Cambridge. In the same year he discovers that black holes could leak energy and particles into space, and even explode in a fountain of high-energy sparks. His breakthrough discovery is published in the journal Nature, in a paper entitled Black hole Explosion?

- 1977 appointed professor of gravitational physics at Cambridge

- 1979 Appointed Lucasian professor of mathematics at Cambridge (a chair held by Sir Isaac Newton in 1663). Elected as a fellow of the Royal Society

- 1982 Awarded a CBE by the Queen.

- 1988 Publishes A Brief History of Time: From the Big Bang to Black Holes, a classic introduction to today's most important scientific ideas about the cosmos. Recorded in the 1998 Guinness Book of Records as an all-time bestseller.

- 1993 Publishes Black Holes and Baby Universes, and other Essays, a collection of scientific articles exploring ways in which the universe may be governed

## Timeline

- **1998** Publishes Stephen Hawking's 'Universe: The Cosmos Explained', a book about the basis of our existence and of everything around us

- **November 2001** releases 'Universe in a Nutshell' in the United Kingdom, a book that unravels the mysteries of recent breakthroughs in physics

- **September 2002** in this year, 'On the Shoulders of Giants', 'The Great Works of Physics and Astronomy', an exploration of some of the greatest visionaries in the history of science including Copernicus, Kepler, Galileo, Newton and Einstein was released

  Publishes 'The Theory of Everything: The Origin and Fate of the Universe', a book that presents the most complex theories of physics past and present.

- July 2004 in this year, Hawking announces that he has solved the Black Hole paradox, which has been a troubling scientists for years.

  He presents his most recent findings at the international conference on general relativity and gravitation in Dublin

Timeline

## Activities

### Class Discussion

What do you know about the universe? When was it formed and what are its contents? Discuss all these facts in class. Note down the points that you did not know.

### Project Work

List the names of 10 scientists. Search the internet and write short paragraphs on them. Also, paste pictures on each one of them. Base your project work on physicists.

### Real Life Observation

Go to your terrace or balcony at night with your mother or sibling. Observe the night sky. What all can you see?

### Questions

1. Who is Stephen Hawking?
2. What is he famous for?
3. When and where was Stephen born?
4. What were his parents' names?
5. What did they do?

6. Describe the uniqueness of the Hawking family? Do you think they were 'eccentric'?

7. Give a brief description of Stephen when he was a young boy?

8. As a college boy, what was Stephen interested in?

9. What subjects did Hawking study at Cambridge after his graduation?

10. Which incurable disease was detected when Stephen was still in college?

11. How did it adversely affect Stephen?

12. When Stephen was doing his PHD, what were his areas of research?

13. With whom did he work with on Albert Einstein's Theory of General Relativity?

14. Name the gadget with the help of which Hawking talks.

15. Name a few books written by Stephen.

16. Enumerate a few occasions where Hawking made public appearances.

17. Name the film made on Hawking.

18. In which television serial did Stephen act in?

# Glossary

**ambitious:** having a strong desire and determination to succeed in life

**Amyotrophic Lateral Sclerosis:** a form of motor neuron disease

**announcement:** a formal public statement about some occurrence

**astronomy:** the branch of science that deals with celestial objects and space

**awkwardness:** the quality of being awkward

**cameo:** a small character part in a play or film which is played by a renowned actor

**celebrity:** a famous person

**communicate:** to share or exchange information, news, or ideas

**dexterity:** skill in performing tasks, especially with the hands

**diagnosis:** the identification or recognition of the nature of an illness

**disabled:** a person having a physical or mental limitation

**eccentric:** a person who is slightly strange

**elementary:** of basic kind

**enlightening:** to give someone great knowledge

# Glossary

**equations:** to equate one thing with another

**fascination:** being too much interested in something

**fixer-upper:** a house that needs repairs

**glittering:** shinning

**gravity:** the force that attracts a body towards the centre of the earth

**groundbreaking:** innovative

**hologram:** a three-dimensional image formed by the interference of light beams from a laser or other light source

**leukemia:** cancer of the blood in which abnormal white blood cells grow in the bone marrow and flood the blood stream

**paralyzed:** to become partly or wholly incapable of any kind of movement

**parasitology:** the branch of biology or medicine concerned with the study of parasitic organisms

**predicament:** a difficult and unpleasant situation

**researcher:** a person who carries out some academic or scientific research

**rudimentary:** elementary or introductory

**slurred:** to speak unclearly or in a manner that the sounds run into one another

## Glossary

**speech synthesizer:** a computer used to produce artificial speech

**submarine:** a vessel, or ship, that can go underwater; these are basically used by military or scientists

**thermodynamics:** the branch of physical science that deals with the relations between heat and other forms of energy

**tracheotomy:** a slit in the windpipe made to relieve an obstruction to breathing

**triumphs:** a great victory

**virus:** an infective agent